To: _____

From: _____

Date: _____

Message: _____

D1608175

_____

_____

_____

This coupon is good for one:

Breakfast in bed

This coupon is good for one:

a manicure by the kids/family

This coupon is good for one:

a day of no bickering

This coupon is good for one:

a shoulder massage

This coupon is good for one:

free hugs

This coupon is good for one:

an afternoon together at the park

This coupon is good for one:

a cup of tea/coffee from your favorite spot

This coupon is good for one:

a new tree planted in your honor

This coupon is good for one:

a picnic in the park prepared by your kids/family

No.1 Mom

This coupon is good for one:

a self-portrait made by me

Love you Mom

This coupon is good for one:

unlimited kisses

This coupon is good for one:

one task of your choice

This coupon is good for one:

a ðvice free day

This coupon is good for one:

weeding the flower beds

This coupon is good for one:

mowing the back yard

This coupon is good for one:

planting herbs for the kitchen

This coupon is good for one:

sweeping the sidewalk

This coupon is good for one:

one-hour massage at your favorite place

This coupon is good for one:

a full day at the spa

This coupon is good for one:

a nice dinner out at the restaurant of your choice

This coupon is good for one:

a bath products shopping spree

This coupon is good for one:

a weekend trip to the destination of your choice

This coupon is good for one:

Mom's choice

This coupon is good for one:

pedicure at your favorite place

This coupon is good for one:

a family afternoon or evening out to the movies

(you choose the flick!)

This coupon is good for one:

date-night with dad

This coupon is good for one:

a family walk

This coupon is good for one:

reading time for you

This coupon is good for one:

the chore of your choice

This coupon is good for one:

uninterrupted bubble bath

This coupon is good for one:

an afternoon all to yourself

This coupon is good for one:

a foot rub

This coupon is good for one:

a family day of service to those in need

This coupon is good for one:

a complete house cleaning by the kids/family

This coupon is good for one:

movie night at home

(you pick the movie)

This coupon is good for one:

one week free of dish duty

This coupon is good for one:

my bed made for a week without having to be asked

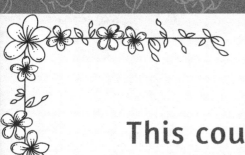

This coupon is good for one:

a family day of random acts of kindness to others

This coupon is good for one:

a cup of coffee or tea brought to you in bed

This coupon is good for one:

Sunday brunch out at the restaurant of your choice

This coupon is good for one:

_____

_____

This coupon is good for one:

This coupon is good for one:

This coupon is good for one:

This coupon is good for one:

This coupon is good for one:

This coupon is good for one:

This coupon is good for one:

This coupon is good for one:

This coupon is good for one:

Made in United States
North Haven, CT
06 May 2022

18961089R00057